FAT CAT

The Steve Mnuchin Story

Rebecca Burns

and

David Dayen

WASHINGTON D.C.

Published in the United States by Strong Arm Press, 2018

www.strongarmpress.com

ISBN-13: 978-1-947492-21-9
ISBN: 1-947492-21-7

Contents

PROLOGUE: MAKING A #MAGABOMBER

On October 22, a couple weeks before the 2018 midterm elections, news reports started streaming in about pipe bombs addressed to prominent Democrats, including former presidents Obama and Clinton, Senators Cory Booker and Kamala Harris, and top donors Tom Steyer and George Soros. Days later, police in south Florida arrested a man in connection with the case.[i] His name was Cesar Sayoc.

His van, which doubled as his home, was a shrine to Donald Trump. It was plastered with bumper stickers supporting the president and condemning CNN, also a recipient of a pipe bomb. Social media posts showed the man physically threatening Trump's personal enemies. Videos of Trump rallies featured the man, something of a MAGA folk hero, flexing and preening for the cameras. After a lifetime detached from politics (he had never even registered to vote until 2016) Sayoc fell under Donald Trump's spell.[ii] Eventually, Sayoc's devotion led him to commit violence against those who he believed had sullied his hero's good name.

The ensuing frenzy to learn more about the mystery bomber uncovered at least one cause for his instability. It turned out Donald Trump wasn't the only real estate impresario to dupe Cesar Sayoc. In 2007, Sayoc refinanced a mortgage he bought a year earlier into a

$385,500 adjustable-rate loan from IndyMac Bank, a notorious subprime lender which would eventually fail and slip into FDIC conservatorship. Within two years, on January 7, 2009, IndyMac Bank filed for foreclosure against Sayoc.[iii] The case docket indicates that Sayoc never even received notice of this lawsuit; the summons was returned unserved in February.

Records from the foreclosure case reveal a backdated assignment of mortgage to IndyMac, dated January 23, sixteen days after the filing of foreclosure. Erica Johnson-Seck, a notorious "robo-signer," affixed her signature to the document. Johnson-Seck would later admit in a deposition that she spent a total of 30 seconds with the documents she signed. She acknowledged that she failed to read them, never learned who inputted the information on them, or signed them in the presence of a notary.

In 2009 - and, indeed, still today - judges could care less about sketchy signatures and phony mortgage assignments. As for Sayoc, he didn't even know his home was being taken from him, so how could he know to fight it? According to the docket, Circuit Court Judge Robert Fogan ruled for summary judgment for IndyMac on September 2, 2009.[iv] In November, the house was bid upon and sold.

By that time, IndyMac had passed out of the FDIC's care. It had a new name - OneWest Bank - and a new owner - a hedge fund manager named Steven Mnuchin. The ten-year odyssey that followed Sayoc's foreclosure and eventual eviction led him to move back in with his mother, and then into his van. He popped steroids, performed as a DJ at strip clubs, and eventually latched onto Trump - someone he would literally kill for. But when Trump got into office, the person he appointed as his treasury secretary was Steve Mnuchin, the man who foreclosed on Cesar Sayoc's home.

It's highly doubtful Sayoc knew much about this when he allegedly sent bombs through the mail. But Sayoc's story shows how a combination of ignorance and partisan passions can make people believe their assailants are their saviors. And it shows how the toxicity of the foreclosure crisis upended millions of lives and reverberated in unforeseen directions.

A multitude of factors turned Cesar Sayoc into a #MAGABomber; it would be foolish to single out Steven Mnuchin for blame. But it's no stretch to say that when catastrophe, suffering, and pain strikes ordinary Americans, Mnuchin often seems to be flitting around the edges of the frame.

CHAPTER 1: TROUBLE IN WESTWOOD

Two months after the Trump administration pulled off one of the biggest wealth transfers in U.S. history, Treasury Secretary Steve Mnuchin gave a public lecture on economic policy at UCLA. To his apparent surprise, it did not go well.

Mnuchin was a key architect of the GOP's $1.5 trillion tax cuts, passed in December, which over the next decade will funnel 83 percent of its benefits to the top 1 percent of U.S. earners -- including to himself. With a net worth of half a billion dollars,[v] Mnuchin and his wife are in the top one-one hundredth of one percent.[vi]

Arriving on UCLA's leafy campus, he was greeted by student protesters who had dressed as Marie Antoinette and were serving cake to passersby. It was a nice touch, but the dramatization was hardly necessary: Mnuchin's own performance quickly betrayed him as a man as aggressively out of touch with his audience as an 18th-century monarch staring down starving peasants.

Introduced as a man who is "a financier in his DNA"--a reference to his Goldman Sachs pedigree--Mnuchin looked taken aback when his arrival on stage drew hisses from the audience. "This is a new experience for me," he said petulantly. "I usually go speak to people who want to listen to me speak."

Nonetheless, Mnuchin pressed on with his standard talking points about tax reform. After years of stagnant wages, he proclaimed, more than 4.5 million workers were finally getting a boost this year thanks to the Tax Cuts and Jobs Act. Not an actual raise, mind you, but the one-time bonuses that Republicans have been touting relentlessly since December. Never mind that the handful of $1,000 checks given out by large companies amount to a fraction of their tax cuts savings, or that most workers at the bottom of the bracket will pay more in taxes by 2027, regardless of whether they ever get a raise. Let them eat one-time bonuses.

The audience continued their subdued heckling and, after about five minutes, Mnuchin began to unravel. "Who hissed?" he snapped awkwardly.

"Can I at least get a hand on who hissed on that one?"

"If you were getting paychecks in February, when your withholdings went down, you wouldn't be hissing."

About seven minutes in, the peasants began revolting. One person screamed that the tax bill was "the politics of cruelty" and was carried out by security. Matters grew even worse when Mnuchin's interlocutor for the conversation, *Marketplace's* Kai Ryssdal, took a shot at the aforementioned bonuses, asking, "What would you rather have? Would you rather have a one-time bonus or a consistent wage increase over the next couple of years?" Mnuchin accused the public radio host of bias. "For people who are getting these thousand-dollar bonuses, these are not crumbs," the multi-millionaire protested.[vii]

All of this culminated in a comically preventable PR disaster for Mnuchin: he tried to block UCLA from releasing video of the event.[viii] Of course, this had the opposite effect of ensuring that the otherwise low-profile incident remained in the news cycle for weeks. After several news organizations filed public-records requests, the university posted the video nearly three weeks later, saying that it had received Mnuchin's consent.[ix] The massive, unforced error seems to have been caused only by the treasury secretary's vanity.

One might expect that a man who posed,[x] smirking, with a sheet of newly minted $1 bills--and delighted at the inevitable comparison to a James Bond villain--might be more prepared to own his overwhelming unpopularity.[xi] But this isn't the first time that Mnuchin has shrunk from the spotlight turned on him through his own immiserating policies.

As chairman of OneWest Bank, Mnuchin began having his address scrubbed from the Internet after anti-foreclosure protesters marched on his 9-bedroom, 10-bathroom Bel-Air mansion in 2011.[xii]

"Without the ... large LAPD presence on scene, I do not think the protest would have been as placid as it was," Mnuchin pled in a 2014 divorce filing in which he asked the judge to keep his address private. "I can only imagine the psychological harm that would have come to our minor children if they were at the house to see over 100 people protesting at their home."[xiii]

Never mind that the victims of OneWest's operation included seniors reportedly foreclosed on over $0.27, and a family with young twin sons evicted abruptly while still in the process of applying for a loan modification.[xiv] Won't someone please think of the children?

Stories like these earned Mnuchin, who ran OneWest from 2009 to 2015, the nickname "Foreclosure King." This apparently wounded him: During his confirmation hearings, he complained to senators that he has "been maligned as taking advantage of others' hardships in order to earn a buck. Nothing could be further from the truth."[xv]

This kind of self-righteous indignation might be no more than a bit of political theater on the part of someone used to getting his hands dirty. But it's equally possible that over the course of a preternaturally fortunate career, built through no discernable virtue of his own, Steven Terner Mnuchin has grown an extraordinarily thin skin.

Born into Wall Street royalty, Mnuchin ascended easily from a job in the mortgage department of Goldman Sachs into the brave new early-aughts world of hedge funds. There, he assembled a consortium of investors to buy a bank that was imploding (thanks to the type of financial products he peddled for years at Goldman) and proceeded to run that bank abominably for a few years before selling it to a bigger bank at enormous profit. A series of train wrecks, in other words, from which he has always managed to jump clear.

That trajectory inspired one of Senator Elizabeth Warren's better quips. "Steve Mnuchin is the Forrest Gump of the financial crisis," she said in a statement after his appointment was announced in November 2016.

Indeed, like the Best Picture-winning tale of Tom Hanks' humble everyman, Mnuchin's story has a compelling sense of continuity to it. The 1994 film starts and ends with the image of a white feather floating through the air; Mnuchin got his own, slightly less whimsical, recurrence when the same protesters who marched on his Bel-Air mansion in 2011 returned on a bleak January day in 2017, the day before his confirmation hearings, carrying signs that read "Stop Trump's Foreclosure King."

They were led by Rose Gudiel, a homecare worker who fought a years-long battle with OneWest to save the Los Angeles home where she lives with her parents, husband and young daughter. The trouble began in 2009, when the family missed a mortgage payment following the devastating murder of Gudiel's brother. Two weeks later, the family got the money together and attempted to send in the payment, but OneWest refused to accept it and started the foreclosure process. The bank relented only after the 2011 protest at Mnuchin's house.

"Mnuchin doesn't care about ordinary people," Gudiel told the rain-soaked crowd six years later.

What's more, Mnuchin doesn't appear to understand just how many ordinary people revile him and the ongoing economic ruin he represents in their lives. In comparison to some of the career white supremacists on the Trump team, the confirmation of "hedge fund guys" like Mnuchin was welcomed in some quarters as a moderating force: He's been described in our papers of record as "pragmatic"[xvi] and "non-ideological." It's possible, given the treasury secretary's shock at his cold reception at UCLA, that even he believes himself to be a clear-eyed technocrat rather than a Wall Street ideologue.

But the intense condemnation from people like Gudiel, or Los Angeles county health worker Robert Strong, who left a bag of horse manure on the secretary's doorstep on Christmas Eve with the note "We're returning the 'gift' of the Christmas tax bill... Warmest wishes, The American people,"[xvii] suggests that most of us understand exactly which side Mnuchin is on--even if he himself does not.

CHAPTER 2: THE PRINCE OF WALL STREET

To hear him tell it, Steven Mnuchin's story is one of humble beginnings. He "started on a folding chair" at Goldman Sachs, as he put it in a January statement to Senators considering his confirmation. "Nine years later, and after many sleepless nights," he wrote, "I was put in charge of Mortgages, U.S. Government Bonds, and Municipal Securities."

That hardly qualifies as a Cinderella story to begin with, but Mnuchin conveniently declined to mention the family connections that made his meteoric rise more or less a foregone conclusion. His father, Robert Mnuchin, was a legendary Goldman Sachs partner who headed up the firm's trading division in the 1970s.[xviii] His brother, Alan Mnuchin, was also a 12-year Goldman veteran, arriving at the firm a few years ahead of the younger Steven.[xix] Even going back another generation doesn't do much to dial up the rags-to-riches factor: Whereas Hillary Clinton can trot out a Scranton factory-worker grandfather, Mnuchin's grandpa was an attorney who co-founded a yacht club in the Hamptons.

Thanks to this elite lineage, even the treasury secretary's early days are a veritable who's who of Wall Street. After graduating from a rarefied New York prep school in 1981, Mnuchin headed off to Yale (where, incidentally, his father was also an alumnus).[xx] There, Steven lived in the posh off-campus Taft Hotel, once inhabited briefly by the 27th commander-in-chief--an early lesson, perhaps, that simply being rich can secure you proximity to the presidency. Mnuchin's two roommates, according to a February 2017 article in the university publication *The New Journal,* were Eddie Lampert and Benjamin Bram, both of whom--you guessed it--went on to work at Goldman Sachs.[xxi]

Lampert later founded his own hedge fund that, at its peak, managed more than $15 billion in investments, including a controlling stake in the struggling retailer Sears.[xxii] Once hailed as "the next Warren Buffett," Lampert has now fallen on a billionaire's version of hard times, but Mnuchin's Treasury appointment gives him a king in his corner. [xxiii]

Some background here helps: After acquiring and combining Sears and Kmart in 2005, the Ayn Rand-loving Lampert sold off thousands of stores without reinvesting in the company, essentially treating it "like an ATM machine" while revenues tanked, according to the former CEO of Sears Canada.[xxiv] Under the control of ESL Investments, the Sears pension fund also grew a $2.1 billion hole. In recent years, "Crazy Eddie" has lent Sears hundreds of millions of dollars as a last-ditch effort to keep the company solvent, but it's still staring down bankruptcy.

If that happens, a little-known federal agency called the Pension Benefit Guaranty Corporation will have a say in who gets repaid first: Lampert, or 200,000 Sears pensioners.[xxv] And wouldn't you know who gets a seat on that three-person board, but the treasury secretary--who, in this case, also happens to have served on the board of Sears for 12 years, after dutifully investing $26 million in his old Yale roommate's fund.[xxvi] Go Elis!

(Mnuchin has said that he plans to divest his position in ESL Investments and recuse himself from any pension decisions involving Sears, but there is little oversight to ensure he follows through.)[xxvii]

This kind of synchronicity, all too common in the world of the super-rich, helps illustrate why Mnuchin's current position is so dangerous to the rest of us. He's spent his entire life rubbing elbows with the people who crashed the economy, precipitated millions of foreclosures and continue to gut worker pensions. In fact, he was one of those people himself. The Treasury Department, with its myriad opaque but consequential functions, provides him no shortage of ways to provide life rafts for Mnuchin's aristocratic pals whenever the mood strikes him, to the detriment of those of us who didn't have the privilege of bunking with him at the Taft Hotel.

But let's return for now to the young Mnuchin's budding career as a financier. The future hedge-fund manager first honed his craft at the *Yale Daily News,* where, as publisher, he pushed to maximize profit by cutting back on content, according to a colorful account in *The New Journal.*[xxviii] Angry editorial staffers attempted a coup, but Mnuchin reportedly quashed it with the help of the newspaper's lawyer.

"I knew Steve Mnuchin back when his idea of fun was starving the Yale Daily News of resources to pad his resume as publisher," Dan Froomkin, a former *News* editor and Mnuchin's contemporary at Yale, tweeted following his appointment.

Classmate Mark Danziger put it more succinctly in an August 2016 *Businessweek* profile. He said he once told Mnuchin, "You put the douche in fiduciary."

But Mnuchin's most important education, it seems, came from the summer internships at the investment bank Salomon Brothers--a rumspringa of sorts before he inevitably rejoined his family at Goldman. Later dissolved into Citigroup, the Salomon of the 1980s was a storied firm with a reputation for high-risk, high-reward trading, including Wall Street's first mortgage finance department.[xxix]

This led to the first of Mnuchin's "Forrest Gump" moments. His mentors at Salomon were Lew Ranieri and Michael Mortara, the iconic figures who pioneered Wall Street's audacious effort to turn mortgages, the sleepy, fixed-rate standby of the 9-to-3 community banker, into a high-risk tradable instrument. Salomon Brothers and friends busily built out this new market during the three summers Mnuchin spent as a trainee, relying in large part on Ranieri's talent for bending politicians to his will. The goal was to allow investment banks to pool mortgages by the thousands, package them into securities, and sell them to investors. Previously this market for mortgage-backed securities was restricted to quasi-governmental giants Fannie Mae and Freddie Mac; Wall Street wanted in on the action.

Ranieri first wrangled Freddie Mac into backing a bond deal that repackaged mortgages issued by a struggling savings and loans institution; Freddie's involvement meant the deal could bypass a number of regulatory regulations. Next, he went to work removing these restrictions permanently. In September 1984, as Mnuchin concluded his Salomon internship and headed back to Yale for his senior year, Congress passed the Secondary Mortgage Market Enhancement Act (SMMEA). The law preempted state-level restrictions and gave investment banks the green light to sell mortgage-backed securities without a government guarantee, paving the way for their proliferation. President Reagan signed SMMEA that October; Ranieri showed up for the ceremony.

Salomon Brothers fired Ranieri in 1987, but his former traders-- Mortara and Mnuchin among them--carried his innovations to other leading investment banks, cementing the mortgage finance business as a mainstay of Wall Street. Ranieri later repented, telling *Fortune* in 2009, "I wasn't out to invent the biggest floating craps game of all time, but that's what happened."[xxx]

Mnuchin, by contrast, would go on to defend securitization as "an extremely positive development in terms of being able to finance different parts of the economy and different businesses efficiently."[xxxi]

After Mnuchin graduated and settled in at Goldman in 1985, Mortara soon followed to help the firm beef up its own mortgage-backed securities division.[xxxii] That put Mnuchin, according to a May 2016 *Bloomberg* report, "front and center for the advent of instruments like collateralized debt obligations and credit default swaps," the dynamite for the world-imploding financial crisis to come.[xxxiii]

Whether he earned this ringside seat, even by Wall Street standards, is another question. While Mnuchin rose steadily through the ranks at Goldman, some of his colleagues suspected that this had little to do with his own merits. His promotion to partner in 1996 came at the expense of Kevin Ingram, a black trader from a working-class background who had gotten an engineering degree from MIT before landing at Goldman. Ingram "was livid," a former colleague tells author William D. Cohan in the 2011 book *Money and Power: How Goldman Sachs Came to Rule the World.* "He was much smarter than Steven, had accomplished a lot more, but his dad wasn't Robert Mnuchin."

This brings us to an important theme, to which we'll return later: Even Mnuchin's fellow political travelers frequently underscore that he is not the sharpest knife in the Cabinet. For example, in a March FOX News interview he urged Congress to give President Trump the power to veto line items on future spending bills. The Supreme Court has previously ruled this unconstitutional, forcing the host to explain sheepishly to Mnuchin that Congress cannot just ignore the court's ruling, because that's not how the whole "checks and balances" thing that we learn about in eighth grade works.[xxxiv] A Yahoo Business profile claims that Mnuchin's former Goldman colleagues consider him "if not especially book smart, then street-savvy,"[xxxv] but let's be honest--it's exceptionally difficult to imagine him being either.

Luckily for Mnuchin, intelligence is no obstacle when you have massive, unearned privilege on your side. Accounts differ on why he left Goldman, but in 2003 he took a position running a hedge fund for George Soros that focused on buying up risky bonds.[xxxvi] A year later, Soros helped Mnuchin launch his own hedge fund which, being a man of the people, he named "Dune Capital" after a spot near his vacation home in the Hamptons.[xxxvii]

While Mnuchin's 2016 nomination announcement described him as the co-CEO of "one of the country's premier investment firms," that's not quite true, as *Forbes'* Kate Vinton reported: "Dune Capital Management, a hedge fund that had $2.5 billion in assets in 2006, filed papers with the U.S. securities regulator to shut down in 2013. It's difficult, if not impossible, to be a premier investment firm today if, as the filing indicates, Dune Capital Management returned funds to investors three years ago."[xxxviii]

Dune did, however, give Mnuchin the vehicle he needed to explore his creative side. When Robert Mnuchin retired from Goldman Sachs, he became a well-respected art dealer. Steven went slightly lower-brow, using Dune to become a major Hollywood producer, by investing hundreds of millions in films such as "The Devil Wears Prada," the "X-Men" franchise and "Avatar."

This might sound like a highly skilled endeavor; the partnership with Dune Entertainment was seen as "one of the most successful alignments of Hollywood and Wall Street," according to the *Wall Street Journal*.[xxxix] But "success" is a subjective term here, of course. Mnuchin is also the man we have to thank for "American Sniper," "Suicide Squad," and the "Entourage" movie, among other cultural and factual low points. Mnuchin wasn't a talent-spotter reading spec scripts in the hopes of unearthing gems; his firm just sprayed money at practically anyone with a camera, getting lucky a few times and at other points turning the stomachs of movie-goers nationwide. In addition to more than 40 executive producer credits, Mnuchin even snagged a (non-speaking) acting part, as a Merrill Lynch exec named Steve Mnuchin in the 2016 film "Rules Don't Apply."[xl]

That's not the only way Mnuchin managed to give Hollywood a little of the Wall Street treatment. As a co-owner and board member of a company called Relativity Media, Mnuchin was named as a defendant in a fraud suit brought by RKA Film Financing, which lent $81 million to help Relativity finance five films. The suit was dismissed with prejudice by the New York Supreme Court in March, meaning that it can't be re-filed. But it essentially alleged that Mnuchin and his colleagues pulled a Big Short on some film nerds: Investors in Relativity were led to believe that it was a "low-risk lending facility," the suit claimed, but later discovered that the cash "was always intended" to pay salaries and corporate expenses and bail out other investors. In May 2015, one of those other investors-- Mnuchin's OneWest Bank--took $50 million out of the studio. Soon after, Relativity filed for bankruptcy.

Even so, churning out blockbusters (and some notable flops) probably clocks in as one of the least objectionable things that Mnuchin has done--notwithstanding an incident that got him into hot water with the government ethics office. During a March 2017 interview with Axios, Mnuchin was asked for movie recommendations.

"I'm not allowed to promote anything that I'm involved in," the treasury secretary said. "So I just want to have the legal disclosure, you've asked me the question, and I am not promoting any product. But you should send all your kids to 'Lego Batman.'"

CHAPTER 3: THE KING OF FORECLOSURES

Mnuchin's biggest coup, and the start of his reign as foreclosure king, came in 2009. In a generous deal with the FDIC, Mnuchin led an investment team that bought the predatory lender IndyMac, saddled with tens of thousands of failing mortgages, for $1.65 billion.[xli] The FDIC had a standard deal for buyers of crisis-era banks; they would cover all losses above the first 20 percent on loan defaults.

Mnuchin, who became CEO and later chairman, treated this as a money-printing machine: his bank, renamed OneWest, could foreclose on homeowners, harvest fees for appraisals and inspections and late payments, and get protected by a federal backstop.

The FDIC lost at least $13 billion on IndyMac; the bank made $3 billion in profits in the five years after it was purchased by Mnuchin and company, much of that coming directly from the FDIC in loss-sharing costs. In 2014, CIT Group announced an agreement to acquire OneWest Bank for $3.4 billion. For six years of ownership, Mnuchin's personal payout was a reported $10.9 million.

According to a *Wall Street Journal* analysis, Mnuchin's predatory lender OneWest Bank started foreclosure proceedings on some

137,000 homes nationwide between early 2009 and the middle of 2015.

The *Journal* obtained a 2011 letter addressed to the FDIC, other regulators and lawmakers, from individuals who said they were former OneWest employees. They claimed the bank "actually makes more money by foreclosing than they would if they allow loan modification." The letter also said OneWest's loan-modification staff "routinely shreds loan modification applications" and lied to homeowners when they called the bank.

This jibes with reports from employees at other major mortgage servicers. A 2009 report by the National Consumer Law Center documented the perverse incentives created by lawmakers and regulators that rendered it more profitable for servicers to foreclose on struggling homeowners, recouping losses quickly and harvesting fees to boot, than to offer a modification.[xlii] OneWest was far from the only bad apple in a rotten system. But Mnuchin's personal connection to thousands of foreclosures secured him a spot in the top tier of reviled Trump nominees.

Mnuchin's foreclosure victims, in particular, were shocked that he had been chosen to lead the Treasury Department. "When he was nominated, it was like the floor crashed underneath me," said Heather McCreary, whose family was evicted from their Sparks, Nevada home in 2010. "It brought back everything. His name was on my paperwork."

Senate Democrats trained some of their limited firepower on Mnuchin. They attempted to present homeowners like McCreary as witnesses at Mnuchin's confirmation hearing, but were denied by Senate Finance Committee Chair Orrin Hatch.[xliii] Instead, a group of senators led by Sen. Elizabeth Warren (D-Mass.) organized a separate forum to hear testimony from McCreary and several other foreclosure victims two days before the official hearing.[xliv]

A TV advertising campaign that also ran in Nevada, Arizona, and Iowa prior to the hearings featured Lisa Fraser, a widow who says Mnuchin's predatory lender "lied to us and took our home" of 25 years, right after her husband's funeral.[xlv]

But in a defiant opening statement to his hearing, Mnuchin cast himself as a tireless savior for homeowners after scooping up failed lender IndyMac. "It has been said that I ran a 'foreclosure machine,'" he said. "I ran a loan modification machine."

Saying that he was no longer affiliated with the CIT Group and lacked access to relevant information, Mnuchin declined to answer a number of specific questions from Senators about OneWest's record-- including the number of foreclosures it initiated, and allegations that the bank had violated HUD and FHA servicing rules. He instead repeated the fuzzy claim that the bank had offered some 101,000 loan modifications to customers nationwide from 2009 to 2013.

The problem is, this only refers to the number of trial modifications *offered*; it says nothing about whether OneWest made them permanent. It comes from a 2013 Treasury Department report which also notes that only 36,000 of the modifications were active, meaning that two-thirds of the offers didn't go through.[xlvi] And even that number doesn't account for borrowers who received modifications and later went into default anyway, due either to the limited terms of the modification or the kind of loan servicing abuses of which OneWest stands accused.

Take Heather McCreary, who herself received one of the 101,000 modifications touted by Mnuchin. She had been laid off from her job as a home health care provider in 2009, and she and her family sought a modification from OneWest as they recovered from the lost wages.

At the Senate Democrats' forum, McCreary explained that the relief was short-lived. After six months of making modified payments, the bank denied McCreary's personal check, claiming that the payment had to be made by cashier's check. "I looked at the paperwork, and couldn't find that on there," McCreary said. "The Legal Aid person working with us couldn't find it."

OneWest told McCreary to re-apply for the modification twice, then cut off all communications and refused to accept payments. "A few months later we had a foreclosure notice taped to the window, with two weeks to get out," she said. The bank was pursuing foreclosure while negotiating a modification — a practice known as dual tracking that is now illegal. The family was evicted in September 2010.

Other testimonials show OneWest to be among America's most creative foreclosure artists, constantly finding different ways to trap their customers and separate them from their homes.

Tara Inden, an actress from Hollywood, California, couldn't get a loan modification from OneWest after multiple attempts.[xlvii] Even after finding a co-tenant willing to pay off her amount due, OneWest refused the money and pursued foreclosure. Inden fended off four different foreclosure attempts, including one instance when she returned home to find a locksmith breaking in to change the locks. "I took a picture of the work order, it said OneWest Bank on it," Inden said. "I called the police, they said what do you want us to do, that's the bank."

OneWest eventually gave her $13,000 as part of the Independent Foreclosure Review, a process initiated by federal regulators forcing OneWest and other banks to double-check their foreclosure cases for errors. Inden received no explanation for why she received the money, but sees it as a tacit admission that OneWest violated the law in her case.

Tim Davis of Northern Virginia had a mysterious $14,479 charge added to his loan's escrow balance on multiple occasions, even after a U.S. Bankruptcy Court ordered it removed. "I don't think that Mr. Mnuchin should be put in a position of government power without further scrutiny," Davis said in an email prior to the treasury secretary's confirmation.

Donald Hackett of Las Vegas claimed in legal filings that OneWest illegally foreclosed on him without being the true owner of his loan.[xlviii] He ended up losing the case, and the home. "They had to cheat to beat me," Hackett alleged. "They came in like union busters to try to bust everybody up and scare you, make you afraid."

Perhaps the worst tale of foreclosure malfeasance from OneWest comes from Teena Colebrook, an office manager from Hawthorne, California, who gained prominence as a Trump supporter disgusted by the Mnuchin selection.[xlix] Her story epitomizes how OneWest saw its customer base as a fortune to be plundered rather than human beings.

Colebrook lost her home to OneWest in April 2015, after a years-long battle that began with the loss of renters who shared the property. Colebrook was informed that the only way she could receive help from OneWest was if she fell 90 days behind on her mortgage payments. This was not true: qualifying for the government's Home Affordable Modification Program, or HAMP, did not require delinquency, only a risk of default.[1]

"They won't tell you in writing and they'll claim they never said that," Colebrook said.

She found fraudulently signed documents in her file, had insurance policies force-placed onto her loan unnecessarily, and kept getting conflicting statements about how much she actually owed. Late fees piled up, like outsized certified mailing costs of $2,000, all appended to her loan. She eventually ran out of appeals. "They wanted my property, wouldn't accept any tender offers," Colebrook said. "They stole my equity. That's why I'm so angry. If [Mnuchin] can't get one person's figures right, how can he be in charge of the Treasury?"

Colebrook put together a complaint group on the Internet to share stories with other sufferers of OneWest. She found multiple people who said they were told to miss payments and then shoved into foreclosure. Others said they were put through year-long trial modifications (under HAMP they were only supposed to be three months long) and then denied a permanent modification, with an immediate demand for the difference between the trial payment and original payment, which could stretch into thousands of dollars. Some lost homes held by their families for decades.

Abuses are still being uncovered: In January, a Miami judge sanctioned OneWest and its attorneys over a "frivolous" foreclosure suit filed against a widow shortly after her husband's death.

Perhaps most shockingly, Mnuchin had the audacity to lie in his written responses to the Senate Finance Committee, claiming that "OneWest Bank did not 'robo-sign' documents," when there is ample evidence that they did.[li]

The robo-signing scandal involved mortgage companies having their employees falsely sign hundreds of affidavits per week, attesting that they had reviewed and verified all the business records associated with a foreclosure — when in fact they never read through the material and just blindly signed off. Those records, in many cases, were prepared improperly, but the foreclosures went ahead anyway because of the fraudulent affidavits.

A mortgage is the biggest financial transaction most people will ever make. The courts have rules ensuring that the decision to take someone's home away is made deliberately, with multiple double-checks and safeguards. The spectacle of robo-signing shows how companies like OneWest just disregarded that obligation and treated foreclosures like a 100-yard dash.

"Did OneWest 'robo-sign' documents relating to foreclosures and evictions?" Sen. Bob Casey, D-Penn., asked Mnuchin as a "question for the record".

Mnuchin replied that "OneWest Bank did not 'robo-sign' documents, and as the only bank to successfully complete the Independent Foreclosure Review required by federal banking regulators to investigate allegations of 'robo-signing,' I am proud of our institution's extremely low error rate."

But even that review [lii]– which was not really so "independent," since the banks hand-picked and paid for their own reviewers [liii]– found that nearly 6 percent of the OneWest foreclosures examined were not conducted properly.

And what sparked that review was a 2011 consent order issued by the federal Office of Thrift Supervision,[liv] which definitively stated that OneWest filed affidavits in state and federal courts "in which the affiant represented that the assertions in the affidavit were made based on personal knowledge or based on a review by the affiant of the relevant books and records, when, in many cases, they were not."

This is the very definition of robo-signing.[lv] Or robo-perjury, if you will, since what we're really talking about is lying to the courts, systematically, on an industrial scale.

Mnuchin's OneWest signed and agreed to the consent order, though it never admitted or denied the activity. However, in at least one Florida foreclosure case, a OneWest employee plainly admitted to robo-signing. On July 9, 2009 – four months after OneWest took over operations from IndyMac, with Mnuchin as CEO – Erica Johnson-Seck, a vice president with OneWest, gave a deposition in which she admitted to being one of eight employees who signed approximately 750 foreclosure-related documents per week.[lvi]

"How long do you spend executing each document?" Johnson-Seck was asked.

"I have changed my signature considerably," she replied. "It's just an E now. So not more than 30 seconds."

Johnson-Seck also admitted to not reading the affidavits before signing them, not knowing who inputted the information on the documents, and not being aware of how the records were generated. And she acknowledged not signing in the presence of a notary. This resulted in false affidavits being submitted in court cases that attempted to take borrowers' homes away.

New York Supreme Court Judge Arthur Schack used the information provided by Johnson-Seck to invalidate OneWest foreclosure cases.[lvii] He also dismissed a separate foreclosure where Johnson-Seck both assigned a mortgage to Deutsche Bank and executed an affidavit on behalf of Deutsche Bank in the same case.

OneWest continued filing sketchy documents for years, even after Johnson-Seck revealed the robo-signing scheme. According to a 2011 Reuters investigation, OneWest issued "foreclosure documents of questionable validity," including filing mortgage assignments that establish ownership of the loan months after the foreclosure action, meaning OneWest (by their own evidence) didn't own the loan at the time they decided to foreclose on the property.[lviii] Similarly, the Columbus Dispatch found dozens of cases in Ohio public records where low-level OneWest employees in Austin, Texas signed off on affidavits attesting to reviewing the underlying loan file, when they had not.[lix]

What this all means is that OneWest effectively stole homes with false evidence, not once but countless times.

Yet Mnuchin blew past this evidence. He doubled down when he re-submitted amended answers for the record to the Senate Finance Committee, once again insisting that OneWest never robo-signed foreclosure documents.

In an August 2017 hearing of the House Financial Services Committee, Rep. Keith Ellison, D-Minn., again raised the issue and confronted Mnuchin with Johnson-Seck's 2009 deposition.[lx]

"I don't think you know what robo-signing is," Mnuchin replied defiantly, insisting there is no legal definition, and denying that there was any robo-signing at OneWest, "for the record."

Federal law prohibits knowingly making false statements to Congress. The Campaign for Accountability, a government watchdog, contends that Steve Mnuchin may have committed that crime on at least three separate incidents when he was asked about OneWest's conduct. The group has asked the Department of Justice to investigate Mnuchin.

"Sec. Mnuchin's dissembling was shameful enough when he served as a CEO, but once he began repeating this obvious untruth to

Congress, Sec. Mnuchin crossed the line into potentially criminal conduct," the watchdog wrote in its August 2017 letter to the DOJ.

Of course, no one is holding their breath for Mark Whitaker to step in.

CHAPTER 4: SCOT FREE

Mnuchin was ultimately confirmed, lies and all, by 53-47, with only West Virginia's Joe Manchin supporting him among Democrats. The vote represented one of the slimmest ever margins for a treasury secretary, but it still meant that Mnuchin would be putting the "douche" in fiduciary at the very highest level.

Most of us probably know little about the Treasury Department, save from what we've gleaned from the Broadway juggernaut "Hamilton." But it's one of the most powerful positions in the government, and the idea that it would serve as a landing place for someone who spent the previous several years swindling people out of their homes is more than a little astonishing. Mnuchin's trials and tribulations may not be the stuff of musicals, but both men did have to overcome some steep odds to achieve their posts.

Therefore we might ask, in the style of the hit hip-hop musical,

How does a rich kid, failson, head of a bank,
Maybe a criminal, who if the Justice Department had done its job
*   might now be*
Locked up in a penitentiary,
go on to be the head of the Treasury?

A big part of this answer has to do with the near-total lack of accountability in the wake of the foreclosure crisis. The apparent ease with which Mnuchin lied through his teeth to Congress says as much about the failures of the Obama DOJ as it does about Trump's. The failure to prosecute the mountain of financial fraud during and after the crisis led those same perpetrators to keep their liberty and their billions, and even invade the highest reaches of the government. For Wall Street scions like Mnuchin, lying has always worked out so far. So why stop now?

Even in an environment of general impunity, Steve Mnuchin appears to have caught some especially lucky breaks. Mnuchin's predatory lender narrowly avoided being sued, according to a 2013 memo from top prosecutors in the California state attorney general's office.

The memo, first obtained by David Dayen in 2017, alleges that One West Bank repeatedly broke California's foreclosure laws.[lxi] Specifically, the bank allegedly rushed delinquent homeowners out of their homes by violating notice and waiting period statutes, illegally backdated key documents, and effectively gamed foreclosure auctions.

In the memo, the leaders of the state attorney general's Consumer Law Section said they had "uncovered evidence suggestive of widespread misconduct" in a yearlong investigation. In a detailed 22-page request, they identified over a thousand legal violations in the small subsection of OneWest loans they were able to examine, and they recommended that Attorney General Kamala Harris file a civil enforcement action against the Pasadena-based bank. They even wrote up a sample legal complaint, seeking injunctive relief and millions of dollars in penalties.[lxii]

But Harris's office, without any explanation, declined to prosecute the case.

State and federal law enforcement have been severely criticized for failing to hold accountable those responsible for the financial crisis and its aftermath. The case provides another example, and this time, the failure to prosecute may have helped the treasury secretary get confirmed.

Knowing that OneWest foreclosed on thousands of California homeowners, the Consumer Law Section first decided to investigate in 2012.[lxiii]

Because of federal pre-emption rules, state prosecutors cannot subpoena national banks for information about their core functions prior to filing a lawsuit. OneWest even tried to obstruct the investigation by ordering its third-party partners to refuse to comply with state subpoenas. But the California attorney general's office was nevertheless able to review over 204,000 publicly available foreclosure documents filed with county recording offices throughout the state, along with other documents purchased from a website called ForeclosureRadar (now called PropertyRadar) that tracks foreclosure activity.

Working through the county records, the attorneys immediately uncovered a startling finding: 86 OneWest documents changing the designation of third-party trustees (SOTs) bore a date prior to March

19, 2009, the date OneWest opened for business. Some dated back to 2008.

"Because it would have been impossible for OneWest to sign the instruments before it became an operational bank," four deputy attorneys general from the Consumer Law Section wrote in the memo, "we deduced that the instruments were backdated." Good deductive reasoning!

The Consumer Law Section also reviewed 913 documents from Quality Loan Service Corp., a trustee that worked with OneWest; 909 of them were backdated. Investigators determined this because metadata showed the documents were created on dates much later than the ones stamped on the documents themselves.

Why did OneWest backdate? So they could foreclose faster.

To understand the importance, one needs to know a bit about California's nonjudicial foreclosure process.[lxiv] If a homeowner misses mortgage payments and no resolution can be worked out, the lender files a notice of default, starting a 90-day clock where the homeowner can either repay the debt or face a sale of their property.

In the original deed of trust that establishes the mortgage, the lender designates a third-party trustee to handle the sale process in case of foreclosure. Lenders can change trustees at any time, memorializing this with a "substitution of trustee" document (SOT).

After the 90 days expire, if the homeowner is still in default, the trustee can record a notice of sale, setting a date for the auction at least

21 days thereafter. The winner of the auction gets the home, and can proceed to evict the homeowner.

But investigators surmised that OneWest listed trustees on notices of default before formally executing the SOTs, then backdated the SOTs to make it look like those trustees were already in place at the time the notice of default was issued.

Had OneWest put the correct date on the SOTs, they would have had to file new notices of default, restarting the 90-day clock and delaying the foreclosure.

"That's consistent with a pattern of creating whatever documents that appear necessary at the time that they're created to grease the wheels of the foreclosure machine," said Mark Zanides, a former federal prosecutor who has represented homeowners in California.

The memo also alleges that OneWest occasionally acted as the loan owner on these SOTs when it was merely the servicer — and therefore did not have the authority to execute the documents. Other SOTs were recorded in county offices without being signed or dated. Trustees acting on OneWest's behalf also did not honor the 90-day waiting period in dozens of instances, issuing the notice of sale prior to the deadline. In other cases, SOTs were never mailed to homeowners notifying them of the identity of the new trustees with the power to sell their homes.

The violations went beyond speeding up foreclosures; investigators also found irregularities with the foreclosure sales. OneWest made or directed others to make "credit bids" at auction, an option only available to the current owner of the mortgage, without executing the required documentation signifying ownership. Not only did this mean the winner of the auction may have made an unlawful bid, but credit bidders were exempt from documentary transfer taxes imposed by cities and counties. Those taxes range from $1.10 to $16.10 for every $1,000 of purchase price.[lxv] Submitting credit bids saved OneWest and its partners from paying the taxes.

Though state investigators could not subpoena OneWest and were obstructed from obtaining more documents, they extrapolated that a full and unencumbered inquiry would yield at least 5,600 violations of foreclosure sale auctions, and turn up instances of backdating in nearly all of the 35,000 foreclosures OneWest had completed in California from 2009 to 2012. They wrote that there would be "substantial public justice value" in such an investigation, which could only proceed through the discovery process of a civil lawsuit. That discovery could have turned up other examples of noncompliance which may have been even more harmful to homeowners.

The attorneys wrote that scrutinizing the scope of OneWest's misconduct would provide public accountability, and enhance the deterrent to violating state foreclosure laws. They hoped to get injunctive relief, forcing OneWest to verify the accuracy of every foreclosure document they issued.

That's on top of civil penalties, which could be up to $2,500 for each violation, and double for "protected classes" like senior citizens or the disabled. Additional restitution could proceed from any premature foreclosures executed as a result of the misconduct.

The case did not contemplate criminal indictments, even though many of the violations described were felonies. While investigators made clear that they expected a tough case, requiring substantial resources and no guarantee of success, the attorneys recommended "that the attorney general authorize us to file a civil enforcement action against OneWest."

Two months later, they were told that the office would not move forward with the complaint. Mnuchin and other OneWest representatives were not even brought in for a meeting to discuss the matter.

This wasn't the first break for Mnuchin's predatory lender. Years earlier, California's Consumer Law division had attempted to investigate OneWest's involvement with reverse mortgages, a product marketed to an especially vulnerable group - elderly individuals and couples on fixed incomes.

Made famous in late-night TV pitches, reverse mortgages let seniors borrow against the value of their homes, to give the elderly a source of income at the end of their lives to make ends meet. But they can turn harmful amid unscrupulous lenders. OneWest's reverse mortgage arm, known as Financial Freedom, gave new meaning to the word "unscrupulous."

After receiving a reverse mortgage, seniors remain responsible for property taxes and homeowner's insurance. When they failed to pay, Financial Freedom often moved quickly to foreclose, without granting repayment options to the borrower.[lxvi] Reverse mortgage loans come due when the home becomes vacant or the owners die; at that point, the family of the borrowers repay the debt, or lenders sell the property to recoup costs. Financial Freedom also reportedly engaged in "widow foreclosures," evicting a spouse from the home after the borrower on the title died.[lxvii]

Data obtained by the California Reinvestment Coalition showed that Financial Freedom was responsible for 39 percent of all reverse mortgage foreclosures since April 2009, yet only 17 percent of all reverse mortgages.[lxviii]

California wanted to investigate this epidemic of Financial Freedom foreclosures. But in January 2010, Mnuchin's OneWest sued successfully to shut down the inquiry. Brian Brooks, the lead lawyer on that 2010 OneWest lawsuit, eventually became OneWest's Vice Chairman.[lxix]

Some of the worst horror stories about OneWest's foreclosure practices involve Financial Freedom reverse mortgages.[lxx] A 103-year-old, Myrtle Lewis, slipped into foreclosure after a one-month lapse in her homeowner's insurance coverage.[lxxi] A 92-year-old widow from Florida was evicted over a 27-cent underpayment.[lxxii]

Sandra Jolley, a whistleblower who eventually filed a whistleblower complaint against Financial Freedom, first fought the company over a reverse mortgage sold to her parents in 2005.

At the time, Jolley's father was dying from terminal cancer and heavily medicated for pain; her mother was in the throes of Alzheimer's disease. A long-term care salesman "knew exactly what he was looking at," according to Jolley, and pushed the couple into a reverse mortgage. She says it was "the last thing they needed." Interest from an investment portfolio covered their bills, and their mortgage was almost paid off. In the meantime, the couple had built up more than $400,000 of equity in the house in Thousand Oaks, California, where they had lived for 35 years.

Through the 2005 reverse mortgage, Financial Freedom paid Jolley's parents a lump sum of $80,000 -- a loan that came due, with fees and interest, when her father died later the same year. Jolley had moved back in with her parents as a caregiver, but did not learn of the loan until after her father's death. That started a protracted legal battle to hang on the house.

After connecting with other consumers, Jolley went on to document more than a dozen ways that Financial Freedom had allegedly violated federal and state regulations, including refusing to allow heirs to repay the loan balance, backdating documents, force placing insurance, and illegally accelerating foreclosure and auction following the death of a borrower.

Jolley says that Financial Freedom repeatedly dodged her attempts to communicate with them and repay the loan. Finally, she says the company sold the house at auction, giving her just two days' notice. The buyer was Colony America--a single-family rental company owned by another member of Trump's inner circle, Tom Barrack. After a year of paying rent on the house her parents used to own, Jolley decided to cut her losses and move away. Her mother died in 2011.

The reverse mortgage "completely destroyed our family," says Jolley. "I didn't have time to grieve my father for six years." A years-long legal battle against Financial Freedom cost nearly $100,000, and "trapped my mother in a two-story house that was unsafe for her, with me as her full-time caregiver, because we couldn't access the equity in our home."

But through her ordeal, Jolley began documenting the depths of abuses in the reverse mortgage industry. She set up a website where reverse mortgage borrowers and their families could contact her and offered them free consultation, often helping others succeed where she had failed. "I learned that Financial Freedom was the absolute worst lender and servicer," says Jolley. "They would sell these things to anyone with a beating heart. And when Mnuchin took over, their aggression only got worse."

In 2014, after amassing hundreds of loan files from Financial Freedom consumers she'd worked with, Jolley filed a federal whistleblower declaration pursuant to the Financial Institutions Reform, Recovery, and Enforcement Act (FIRREA). Passed in the wake of the savings and loan crisis, FIRREA encourages whistleblowers to reveal fraud affecting federally insured financial institutions. (Reverse mortgages, including those initiated and serviced by Financial Freedom are backed by the Federal Housing Administration (FHA) through its Home Equity Conversion Mortgage, or HECM, program.)

The following year, after Mnuchin's OneWest Bank merged with CIT Group, taking Financial Freedom along with it, HUD's Office of Inspector General served the new institutions with subpoenas regarding the reverse mortgage loans, according to the bank's 10-K filings.

It wasn't clear what, if anything, would come of this, until June 2017, when the Justice Department made public an $89 million settlement, alleging that Financial Freedom had ripped off the government by receiving unlawful federal insurance payments on reverse mortgages.[lxxiii] Under its terms, Jolley received $1.6 million for her service.

It was a bit unprecedented - a bank formerly run by Steve Mnuchin, the sitting Treasury Secretary, getting hit with an 8-figure fine for stealing from the government.

According to the settlement, Financial Freedom repeatedly filed insurance claims with the FHA, and received interest payments, without following program guidelines. This gave the company a critical backstop for the reverse mortgages that often harmed borrowers like Jolley's parents.

Under the HECM program, the FHA guarantees repayment to reverse mortgage lenders, including legacy costs of servicing and maintenance. They even collect interest while the claim is being processed, which often takes years. It was the perfect system for Mnuchin's company to use to its advantage. All lenders have to do is follow the guidelines of the program and they cannot lose.

Financial Freedom, according to the settlement, did not meet those regulatory requirements. Specifically, they did not hit deadlines for appraising the property, submitting claim forms, and initiating sales of the homes. And then they falsely claimed to the FHA that they met the deadlines, in order to collect interest payments.

In other words, Financial Freedom didn't spend the money required by the reverse mortgage insurance program, but still recouped interest payments from the FHA. Stealing from the program reduces its solvency and the viability of the reverse mortgage program, which is running a $14.5 billion deficit.

"This lender failed to comply with FHA servicing requirements and sought to receive financial gains that it was not legally entitled to," said Inspector General for the Department of Housing and Urban Development David Montoya, in a statement accompanying the settlement.

The period of Financial Freedom's misconduct covers a period that began shortly after Mnuchin became chair of OneWest and ended shortly after he and his fellow investors sold the company. He was either unaware of the breakdown in controls at Financial Freedom, or aware of the misconduct and allowed it to continue.

OneWest officials have claimed that criticism of their reverse mortgage practices "are really criticisms of the regulations," a laughable alibi that falls apart amid the slightest scrutiny.[lxxiv] Mnuchin claimed during his confirmation hearing that he "was so troubled [by stories of so-called widow foreclosures] that I discussed it with our primary regulator, the Office of the Comptroller of the Currency... Unfortunately, HUD did not see it my way, and we were forced to foreclose on senior citizens even when they only owed $1."

It's true that HUD guidelines established in 2015, aimed at stemming losses in the reverse mortgage insurance fund, made it harder to extend relief. But in an op-ed published in *The Hill* following Mnuchin's hearing, housing and finance experts from the Center for American Progress, the California Reinvestment Coalition and Americans for Financial Reform explained why Mnuchin's attempt to pin the blame solely on HUD was misleading:

This [2015 HUD] policy, which has subsequently changed, was not in place during most of the years Mnuchin led a reverse mortgage servicer and foreclosed on seniors.

In fact, HUD issued this policy just four months before Mnuchin sold OneWest. Under Mnuchin, OneWest had a green light from HUD, to help seniors stay in their homes. It simply chose not to. [lxxv]

The DOJ settlement suggests that Financial Freedom was both ruthless toward borrowers and deceitful toward the FHA. An initial assessment of Financial Freedom's liability put the cost of the violations at over $200 million, so the company likely got off easy with an $89 million settlement.[lxxvi]

In a June 2017 letter to the Financial Services committee, Rep. Maxine Waters, D-Calif. questioned whether the Trump administration's investigation and settlement had been marred by conflicts of interest related to Mnuchin's connection to Financial Freedom:

While the DOJ recently announced a settlement with Financial Freedom, a myriad of questions remain regarding the adequacy and impartiality of this settlement… It is impossible to determine based on the scant details included in the press release whether or not this is a fair settlement. Furthermore, this settlement seems only to resolve claims concerning costs incurred by the federal government, while failing to address at least two sets of serious allegations regarding harms that OneWest inflicted on borrowers.[lxxvii]

Waters' letter also asked for clarification as to whether the HUD Office of Inspector General was continuing its initial investigation.[lxxviii] In August 2017, the OIG issued a final civil action, advising that no further action was required by HUD. But in March the OIG rejected our FOIA request for investigative documents related to Financial Freedom, saying the investigation was ongoing.

While Financial Freedom has stopped initiating new reverse mortgages, the broader problems in the industry continue. HUD data obtained by the California Reinvestment Coalition showed a 646% increase in foreclosures against seniors in 2016.

Last year, Jolley launched her own organization, Consumer Advocates Against Reverse Mortgage Abuse, to advocate for improved regulations.[lxxix] The irony is not lost on her that, five years after the Treasury Department had to give the FHA an emergency cash infusion to cope with losses from federally insured reverse mortgages, Mnuchin now oversees the agency collecting restitution for his former bank's alleged wrongdoing. "It was painful for that $89 million to go the Treasury," says Jolley. "Consumers got nothing."

CHAPTER 5: A WOLF IN WONK'S CLOTHING

Many high-rollers were thrilled to see Mnuchin take the helm at Treasury. The day after his nomination, he took to Fox Business News to call for the privatization of mortgage giants Fannie Mae and Freddie Mac. These New Deal programs, which increase funding available for homeownership for the middle class, have been in the target sights of conservative ideologues practically since their creation, and the last time Wall Street took over mortgage financing the global economy melted down. Yet Mnuchin was undaunted. "We've got to get [Fannie and Freddie] out of government control," he told Fox Business. The companies' shares immediately shot up 30 percent.[lxxx]

John Paulson, the hedge fund guru who has been a key patron of Mnuchin's career, is among those betting on Fannie-Freddie privatization. Mnuchin's financial disclosures later revealed that he himself had $1 - $2 million worth of investments in Paulson's fund when he made his pitch, although he promised to divest his holdings.[lxxxi]

While Mnuchin appears to have since backed off from this proposal, it set the tone for his tenure. It's hardly unusual for the Treasury to be staffed by former banking executives--fellow Goldman alums Robert Rubin and Henry Paulson previously headed the agency-

-but the Mnuchin Treasury looks a bit like a 10-year class reunion for people who precipitated the financial crisis. Much of the early staffing was handled by Jim Donovan, another top Goldman official who Trump nominated as Mnuchin's deputy secretary. Donovan later dropped out, but by the agency's own omission, he played a key role in getting things up and running at Treasury, while still working at Goldman.[lxxxii]

In June 2017, reports circulated that Mnuchin would tap Brian Brooks, the former OneWest vice chairman who fended off an early lawsuit against Financial Freedom, as his #2. When Brooks also withdrew in October, Mnuchin indicated that he was in no hurry to fill the deputy position.

Instead, the secretary has relied instead on "counselors" that do not require confirmation.[lxxxiii] They come from a range of diverse backgrounds, including banks, law firms that represent banks, and the offices of politicians who want to deregulate banks.[lxxxiv] Chief among them[lxxxv] is Craig Phillips, who, as the go-to guy on regulatory reform and housing finance, "certainly knows a thing or two about Fannie and Freddie," writes financial journalist Gretchen Morgenson. Prior to his most recent position at the asset-management firm BlackRock, Morgenson reports, Phillips worked for a series of Wall Street banks, including Morgan Stanley:

As the leader of Morgan Stanley's mortgage desk during the peak mortgage-mania years of 2004 and 2005, he ran the operation that bundled loans and sold them to the two government-sponsored enterprises. When those loans blew up and the government sued Morgan Stanley, Mr. Phillips was a named defendant in the initial case—a case that resulted in the firm paying a $1.25 billion settlement.[lxxxvi]

The White House finally named a deputy treasury secretary, but it was one of Mnuchin's many counselors who had been there all along: Justin Muzinich, described as an "architect" of the administration's tax-cut plan.[lxxxvii] Before settling at Treasury, he worked at Morgan Stanley and an investment fund, Muzinich & Company, founded by his father. So he fits right in.

Perhaps most galling is the appointment of former OneWest CEO Joseph Otting as head of the Office of Comptroller of the Currency, an independent bureau within Treasury that charters, regulates, and supervises all national banks. This put both OneWest CEOs in its short history, prior to being swallowed up by CIT, in key regulatory positions in the government.

A career banker without an advanced degree or any previous government experience, Otting has made no bones about where his sympathies lie. "I like bankers," was his opening line in an April speech before the Independent Community Bankers of America. In what's now standard nomenclature for Trump regulators, Otting went on to describe banks as his "customers," and his own job as improving "responsiveness" to them.[lxxxviii] That responsiveness was on full display when, in the wake of the Wells Fargo fake account scandal, Otting's OCC investigated sales practices at major banks and found over 250 separate problems that needed fixing, including several banks opening accounts in their customers' names without consent.[lxxxix] But OCC refused to make these findings public, instead asking politely that the banks please refrain from lawbreaking if they can help it.

It took just a little over a year for the revolving door to spin back. Drew Maloney, who as legislative affairs liaison for Treasury played a major role crafting both the tax legislation and a law deregulating the banking industry, headed out in June to run the American Investment Council, the trade association for the private equity industry.[xc]

Meanwhile, Mnuchin's Treasury has slashed the staff and funding of the Office of Financial Research, created after 2008 to serve as an early-warning system for future meltdowns.[xci] He has also sidelined the agency's deep bench of economists in the Office of Tax Policy, an apparent function of his disdain for expertise.

This has led to some deeply embarrassing moments: chief among them, the agency's "analysis" of the deficit impact of tax reform. During the debate over the tax bill, Mnuchin recited with religious conviction the claim that the $1.5 trillion overhaul would pay for itself through increased economic growth. Asked to provide any evidence of this, at all, he repeatedly claimed that more than 100 employees were "working around the clock on running scenarios for us."

In late November, as a vote on the bill approached, an anonymous economist at the Office of Tax Policy confirmed what most of us expected by that point: there was no such analysis. The details of what was actually going on, gleaned by the *New York Times'* Alan Rappeport, would almost be funny if they hadn't heralded utter disaster:

Those inside Treasury's Office of Tax Policy, which Mr. Mnuchin has credited with running the models, say they have been largely shut out of the process and are not working on the type of detailed analysis that he has mentioned.

An economist at the Office of Tax Analysis, who spoke on the condition of anonymity so as not to jeopardize his job, said Treasury had not released a "dynamic" analysis showing that the tax plan would be paid for with economic growth because one did not exist.

Instead of conducting full analyses of tax proposals, staff members have been running numbers on individual provisions or policy ideas, like lowering the tax rate on so-called pass-through businesses and figuring out how many family farms would benefit from the repeal of the estate tax.[xcii]

In fact, it's already estimated that just 20 farms a year are subject to any inheritance tax at all--not exactly tough math.[xciii] But even after it was exposed that Mnuchin's corps of number-crunchers were, basically, just chilling and counting sheep, he persisted with the fiction by releasing a one-page, 500-word document and passing it off as the thing we'd all been waiting for. The so-called analysis could have been simplified further by just writing, "trust us."

The document was "embarrassing to all of us," an unnamed senior official told Politico.[xciv]

Of course, it didn't matter in the end--Congress passed a tax bill based on the completely unsupported premise that massive corporate tax cuts will jumpstart the economy. Within a decade, supposedly, the Gross Domestic Product (GDP) will consistently be growing at a rate of 3 percent or higher, up from about 2 percent during the past decade.[xcv]

Watching Mnuchin attempt to argue this is a surreal experience. Consider, for example, the exchange between Mnuchin and Kai Ryssdal at that fateful February UCLA lecture. In the passage that follows, do not be intimidated by economics-speak or let your eyes glaze over. Instead, let it sink in that you may well know just as much economics as the man at the helm of our economy:

Ryssdal: Let me take it to the tax law. [Hissing from audience.] You and the president and the Congress passed last year, the president signed it, it took effect on the first of January, as you know. During your confirmation hearings, you said whatever tax reform the Trump administration is going to work on will not add to the debt and the deficit.

Mnuchin: That's true and I stand behind that. [Hissing from audience.]

Ryssdal: Sir, the tax bill that's enforced now adds a trillion and a half dollars to the deficit.

Mnuchin: No, that's not the case. [Hissing from audience.] The tax bill scored on a static basis adds a trillion and a half — let me just go through the numbers — there is a half a trillion dollars difference between what's called baseline and policy. Those are things that were gonna be extended anyway. That takes the number down to a trillion dollars. We believe that, with 90 basis points of growth, there will be over —

Ryssdal: Why don't you explain what 90 basis points means?

Mnuchin: Ninety basis points of GDP. So GDP going from basically 2.1 percent to 3 percent. And for you math majors in the room, the break even is about 35 basis points.

Ryssdal: So in other words, three-tenths of 1 percent on growth.

Mnuchin: That's correct.

Ryssdal: OK. The catch of course is, and as you know, you did have two quarters of 3 percent economic growth this past year, but year-over-year growth in the American economy was 2.3 percent. So you're still far away from the target, right?

Mnuchin: Absolutely. That's why we're doing all of these things. So these things have some impact. And all of our economic plans are about creating sustained economic growth. [Hissing from audience.]

Fancy terms like "basis point" and solicitous allusions to "the math majors in the room" won't save Mnuchin here. Listen to him speak, and it becomes obvious that while he is desperately trying to appear wonkish, the Coke bottle-glasses and Econ 101 slang are just window-dressing. Underneath them, he is just a man sputtering about doing "things" that will have "impact."

Pretty much everyone else has been forced to admit that the whole 3 percent growth in a decade thing is magical thinking. After being publicly taken to task by their peers, a group of nine conservative economists essentially withdrew their endorsement of the claim with the lame excuse that they hadn't said *when* the 3 percent growth might occur.[xcvi] Yet, almost to his credit, Mnuchin is undeterred: He repeated this line again in a sanguine speech on Tax Day.[xcvii]

Two weeks after that speech, the Bureau of Economic Analysis issued its advance estimate for GDP growth in the first quarter of 2018, the initial three months with the tax cut in place. Growth stood at 2.3 percent,[xcviii] the same figure it's been at for a year; it's since been downgraded to 2.2 percent.[xcix] Second quarter GDP spiked to 4.1 percent, a figure endlessly repeated by Trump and Mnuchin, who told Fox News in July America was "definitely are in a period of four or five years of sustained 3 percent growth at least."[c] But economic experts described the GDP figure more as "the luck of the draw," a temporary condition unlikely to last.[ci]

Meanwhile, the real impact of the tax cut could be found on Wall Street. The nation's top companies have returned $1 trillion to shareholders through stock buybacks over the past year, leaking the corporate windfall out to wealthy investors.[cii] As for workers, in a candid talk at the Dallas Federal Reserve in May, CEOs admitted that they wouldn't be giving out pay raises anytime soon, and that they expected to cut back their workforces.[ciii]

Welcome to the Mnuchin economy.

It's worth noting who actually did the intellectual heavy lifting on tax reform. In the weeks before the administration released its tax outline in April 2017, Mnuchin met with Apple CEO Tim Cook and the executives of a host of other tax-dodging corporations[civ] that are getting deep tax cuts and a reprieve in the form of a one-time, 15.5% tax on profits stashed overseas.[cv] The next month, when the Treasury released its recommendations for further tax regulatory changes, they were almost entirely copied from a U.S. Chamber of Commerce memo on the same subject.[cvi] And when it came to figuring out withholdings under the new tax bill, Mnuchin announced that the IRS would set up an online calculator for workers to check that the right amount of money was being withheld from their paycheck, shifting responsibility from the government to taxpayers.

When it comes to the finer points of fiscal or monetary policy, Mnuchin is immediately out of his depth. But when it comes to sycophancy, he excels--whether it's praising the president's "perfect genes" or carving out an ever-expanding role at the White House. The Treasury building is located right next to the 1600 Pennsylvania Ave, which makes it easy for Mnuchin to pop over whenever he pleases, according to a January report in Politico:

Senior administration officials say that [White House Chief of Staff John] Kelly has been particularly annoyed by Mnuchin's desire to attend as many meetings as possible and participate in photo ops, on the reasoning that all policy matters are tangentially related to Treasury.

"The sanctions led Mnuchin to get more involved in the Iran deal and North Korea, much to the frustration of some of the national security experts," including national security adviser H.R. McMaster and Defense Secretary James Mattis, said a close adviser to the White House. "McMaster and Mattis were like, 'What is this guy doing here? You are not a policymaker here. You should be managing your department and the implementation of the tax bill.'[cvii]

More recently, as part of the team of rivals-esque U.S. trade delegation to China, Mnuchin reportedly locked other Trump officials out of a closed-door meeting and got into a "screaming match" with trade adviser Peter Navarro.[cviii]

But perhaps the peak Mnuchin moment to dominate the news cycle, thus far, involved a familiar activity for the uber-rich Trump cabinet: using their lofty positions to feed at the public trough.

In August 2017, the secretary's actress wife, Louise Linton, posted an Instagram photo of the couple deplaning from a government jet.[cix] The caption doubled as an advertisement for the designers she was wearing:

"Great #daytrip to #Kentucky! #nicest #people #beautiful #countryside #rolandmouret pants #tomford sunnies, #hermesscarf #valentinorockstudheels #valentino #usa."[cx]

The tacky factor jumped when Linton berated an Instagram user who criticized her in the comments. And the incident turned into a full-fledged scandal when it turned out that Mnuchin may have chartered a government plane simply to take his wife to see the solar eclipse. (It would end up being one of a series of allegations of Mnuchin's taxpayer-funded jet-setting: he reportedly requested a $25,000/hour military escort for his honeymoon,[cxi] and cost the government nearly $1 million on plane travel in 2017 alone.)[cxii]

The treasury secretary responded to the eclipse dust-up in characteristically dickish fashion. "People in Kentucky took this stuff very seriously," Mnuchin told the *Washington Post* .[cxiii] "Being a New Yorker, I don't have any interest in watching the eclipse."

A recently obtained photo of Mnuchin and Linton, gazing up at the heavens, says otherwise.[cxiv] ThinkProgress, which got it hands on this smoking gun through a public records request, learned that the U.S. Mint had even procured their eclipse glasses for them.

CHAPTER 6: REGULATORY MELTDOWN

Penny-ante grifting and spectacular gaffes aside, most of the truly troubling things at Treasury are happening out of the spotlight. Mnuchin's special blend of incompetence and ill-intent leaves the field wide open for rampant Wall Street deregulation.

Take, for example, a confounding exchange between Mnuchin and Sen. Elizabeth Warren at a May 2017 Senate Banking Committee hearing.[cxv] Mnuchin indicated that the Trump administration supports a 21st century version of the Glass-Steagall Act, except for the part about separating commercial and investment banks, which is substantially what is meant by Glass-Steagall.

Warren wasn't having it.

Responding to Mnuchin's earlier testimony that the White House didn't support "a separation of banks from investment banks," the Massachusetts senator pointed out that "The president and this administration have repeatedly said that they support a 21st century Glass-Steagall."

Indeed, Mnuchin said these words in his confirmation hearings.[cxvi] Former National Economic Director Gary Cohn has said the same.[cxvii]

And the 2016 Republican Party platform adds explicitly, "We support reinstating the Glass-Steagall Act of 1933 which prohibits commercial banks from engaging in high-risk investment."[cxviii] As Warren said to Mnuchin, "Now you've just said the opposite."

Mnuchin responded that there wasn't any reversal, despite Warren's incredulity. He said that the administration merely supported a 21st-century version of the law. "Which means there are aspects of it, OK, that we think may make sense. But we never said before that we supported a full separation —"

"There are aspects of Glass-Steagall that you support but not breaking up the banks and separating commercial banking from investment banking?" Warren interrupted. "What do you think Glass-Steagall was if that's not right at the heart of it?"

While the Glass-Steagall Act was part of a larger bill, the Banking Act of 1933, which also created the Federal Deposit Insurance Corporation, for about 80 years it's been pretty clear that "Glass-Steagall" refers to the firewall between commercial and investment banking.[cxix] There are no real "aspects" of the policy to pick from without that fundamental structure.

"So--in favor of Glass-Steagall which breaks apart the two arms of banking, except you don't want to break apart the two parts of banking," said Warren. "This is like something straight out of George Orwell."

In fact, it's even more Orwellian than that. Tim Pawlenty, then the head of the industry lobby the Financial Services Roundtable, neatly summarized the situation that month when he told Bloomberg that, when the administration says "21st-century Glass-Steagall," what they really mean is deregulation.[cxx] "The administration's view of a modern-day Glass-Steagall is a two-tiered approach to regulation in which smaller banks would receive some regulatory relief," Pawlenty said.

Of course, partial deregulation for smaller banks has nothing to do with Glass-Steagall at all. But selling deregulation as regulation is the very "through the looking Glass-Steagall" moment the industry has successfully created.

The next month, in June 2017, the Treasury released its first report recommending changes to the financial regulatory system.[cxxi] Compiled with the assistance of 244 different banking industry groups, and often citing or lifting directly from bank lobbyist briefing papers, it identified numerous ways that regulators could go around Congress and significantly undermine the already weakened rules in Dodd-Frank. It's a wish list for deregulation — and most of it can be accomplished under the radar.

In an appendix, Treasury lists the organizations and individuals who provided input to them for the report. Sen. Sherrod Brown's office ran the numbers, finding that Treasury consulted with 14 consumer advocates and 244 banking industry groups, a ratio of around 17-to-1.

Predictably, there's something for every bank of every size, with enough exemptions, reductions, and referrals back to the lowest common denominator to enable the industry to run wild. The report calls for making stress tests and supervision "more transparent," which is code for allowing banks to know when examiners will arrive and how to game the process. It also suggests reduced frequency, with stress tests and living will plans every two years instead of annually. It wants to add multiple exemptions to nearly all capital rules. It also wants all regulators to engage in cost-benefit analysis in rulemaking, a way to bog the process down in bureaucracy — and to set up targets for lawsuits after the rules are written. It wants to roll back mortgage rules put in for borrower protection after a crisis that resulted in millions of foreclosures.

How much of this has Treasury actually accomplished so far? In an April report, the agency boasted that it had already reduced its regulatory agenda by nearly 100 regulations. As with most reports that Mnuchin has had a hand in, the math here is a little unclear. But there are several areas where Treasury or related bodies have already pulled off some dramatic slash-and-burn.

Take the Financial Stability Oversight Council (FSOC), a 10-member body created by Dodd-Frank to identify and constrain risk in the financial system. Although Treasury only has one vote, the secretary chairs FSOC and tends to have outsized sway. In that capacity, Treasury has pushed successfully to change the designation criteria for "systemically important financial institutions" that are subject to enhanced supervision. The process began with a vote to de-designate AIG, freeing the insurance giant from stricter prudential standards a decade after the Fed rescued it from bankruptcy.[cxxii]

"The original test for designation was, 'if a bank got in trouble, would it create a threat to the financial system?'" says Marcus Stanley, policy director for Americans for Financial Reform. "They've changed that to, 'do we think it is likely to get in trouble?' even though the whole point was to regulate banks before they're about to fail."

Treasury also called for loosening capital requirements on banking giants, and the Federal Reserve is dutifully carrying that out with Mnuchin's tacit approval.[cxxiii] This change enables banks to take on more risk without forcing them to maintain a cushion that can be used to pay for any losses. There used to be bipartisan agreement that stronger capital requirements would make for a stronger financial system and prevent taxpayer bailouts.[cxxiv] Or there was, until Trump's team came to town.

The Office of the Comptroller of the Currency (OCC), the ostensibly independent bureau controlled by ex-OneWest CEO Otting, has even greater ability to make far-reaching deregulatory changes. In August 2017, the OCC announced that it was beginning the process of reforming the Volcker rule, another Dodd-Frank regulation that aims to prevent banks that accept taxpayer-insured deposits from making risky market bets. According to Reuters, the changes being considered include shifting the burden of proof for compliance to regulators and narrowing the definition of which funds are considered risky.[cxxv]

This year, the OCC has also proposed amendments to the rules governing banks' leverage ratio, or how much debt they can assume relative to their capital. After lifting a longstanding prohibition on partnerships between national banks and payday lender ACE Cash Express, giving the chain a means to circumvent state-level interest rate caps,[cxxvi] in May the OCC issued guidance essentially encouraging banks to start hawking their own payday loans.[cxxvii] And in July, the

OCC began accepting applications for so-called "fintech" firms - online lenders and other tech companies - to acquire national bank charters, which could immunize them from state consumer protection laws.[cxxviii] The move came hours after Mnuchin's Treasury Department released a report recommending the action.[cxxix]

"It's my viewpoint that consumers should have more choices," said Otting in a press briefing.

What's more, Treasury is already getting help on its deregulatory agenda from Congress--including some Democrats. In May, President Trump signed into law the Economic Growth, Regulatory Relief, and Consumer Protection Act, which will accomplish several of the objectives outlined in the Treasury report. It's known as the Crapo bill, both for co-author and Senate Banking Committee chair Mike Crapo, and as a not-so-subtle commentary on its general quality. Thirty-three House Democrats joined Republicans in voting for the bill. The Senate passed its version in March with the support of 16 Democrats.

Supporters of the bill were taking up a key flag carried by Treasury: freeing community banks from allegedly burdensome regulations. One section of the June report had called for eliminating multiple burdens on small banks and credit unions, raising the exemption thresholds for stress tests, capital and liquidity rules, and supervision.

The Treasury report claimed that community banks and credit unions are being strangled by Dodd-Frank regulations, while citing an unbroken trajectory of small bank closures going back to 1984, 26 years before Dodd-Frank's introduction.

It's not a new rhetorical move: For years, big Wall Street banks have laundered themselves through down-home community banks, with bored Democrats and a bored public helpless to lift the mask.

Under Dodd-Frank, any bank over a $50 billion asset threshold is subject to enhanced regulatory standards administered by the Fed, which include extra capital and liquidity requirements, stress tests, and souped-up risk management.[cxxx] The new law will raise that threshold to $100 billion immediately, and to $250 billion within 18 months. Twenty-five of the 38 biggest domestic banks in the country, and globally significant foreign banks that have engaged in rampant misconduct, would get freed from enhanced supervision.

"Community banks are the human shields for the giant banks to get the deregulation they want," said Elizabeth Warren, who waged a last-minute, uphill fight to stop the bill in the Senate.

Perhaps the worst of these gifts to smaller banks is Section 104, which could aid and abet discriminatory lending. A recent Center for Investigative Reporting study showed that African-Americans still find it far more difficult to get a home loan than whites, even if they have greater income and wealth.[cxxxi] Loans for people of color also often come with higher interest rates and fees.

But the new law will hinder regulators from suing lenders over such practices. Dodd-Frank increased data requirements under the Home Mortgage Disclosure Act, or HMDA, having lenders report credit scores, debt-to-income ratios, loan-to-value ratios, and other information. But Section 104 exempts banks and credit unions from reporting that data if they make fewer than 500 loans per year. This includes 85 percent of all banks and credit unions.

"HMDA data is a crucial tool to make sure every American has access to opportunity," said Katie Porter, a California congresswoman-elect and mortgage industry expert. "Discrimination in lending has an ugly history in the U.S. This would make the data unreliable." And the data are the building blocks of any lending discrimination case; you can't enforce fair housing laws without the facts.

All this is shaping up to be Mnuchin's next "Forrest Gump" moment. He's already grappled with these rules, including the $50 billion regulatory threshold and enhanced data disclosure, from the other side of the revolving door. The 2015 merger of OneWest with CIT, which Mnuchin helped engineer, put the combined institution over that key regulatory threshold, requiring bank officials to clear the unusual hurdle of public hearings staged by the OCC.[cxxxii]

Armed with data on OneWest's foreclosure and banking practices, advocacy groups like the California Reinvestment Coalition (CRC) turned a typically dry, procedural hearing into an indictment of the bank's record. Sandra Jolley and other reverse mortgage victims were among those who testified against the merger, citing OneWest's ownership of sleazy reverse mortgage company Financial Freedom.

"It was probably the largest protest of a bank merger in U.S. history," says CRC's deputy director, Kevin Stein.

Community groups also charged that the bank was failing in its obligations to communities of color--both by locating its branches overwhelmingly in white neighborhoods, and by putting forward a woefully inadequate plan to increase lending in low and moderate-income neighborhoods. One of the factors regulators must consider when banks merge is whether the institutions are meeting the requirements of the Community Reinvestment Act (CRA), a federal law passed in 1977 in response to the history of redlining in black and Latino communities.

As part of its application, OneWest had outlined a plan for $5 billion of lending in low and moderate-income neighborhoods over four years. CRC Executive Director Paulina Gonzalez charged during the hearings that the public subsidies the bank had received from the FDIC and TARP funds "dwarfs the measly CRA plan offered by the bank and dwarfs the public benefit of this merger."

The merger went through regardless. In November 2016, CRC and Fair Housing Advocates of Northern California filed a fair housing complaint with the Department of Housing and Urban Development, alleging that OneWest Bank had engaged in discriminatory lending. According to data submitted by OneWest to federal regulators, black and Latino borrowers were significantly underrepresented in the bank's lending. In 2015, for example, just 8.4% of OneWest's mortgage loans in Southern California went to Latino borrowers, even though they comprised 22.4% of borrowers across the industry and 43% of the area's population.[cxxxiii]

While new loans were few and far between, the majority of OneWest's foreclosures in Southern California took place in neighborhoods of color. "The foreclosure to loan ratio in these neighborhoods was 9:1," notes Stein. The coalition's redlining complaint is still pending with HUD.

Meanwhile, the Community Reinvestment Act is the next major regulation in Treasury's crosshairs. After months of alluding to plans to "modernize" the CRA, in April Treasury released a report proposing sweeping changes to its implementation. Among other suggestions, Treasury wishes to expand the "universe of CRA-eligible activities" and increase the "clarity and flexibility" of CRA examinations, even though banks almost always receive passing grades from regulators as it is. The OCC has taken the lead on rewriting CRA rules, based on Treasury's guidance. Though Trump's other banking regulators have blanched at undermining regulations to ensure low-income communities aren't left behind by the financial system, Otting's OCC is thundering ahead on its own.[cxxxiv]

That this process is happening concurrently with changes to the Volcker rule and leverage ratios means that Mnuchin and Otting are within arm's reach of unraveling the key regulations that hemmed in the bank they ran, albeit insufficiently. All told, Mnuchin's Treasury could easily roll back the clock on not just years, but decades, of reforms.

CHAPTER 7: THE PENDULUM SWINGS BACK

Among the many improbabilities of the Trump administration, it would have been difficult to predict that Steve Mnuchin would simultaneously turn out to be one of its most blundering members--it's a crowded field in that respect--and one of its most effective.

Under normal circumstances, this might seem contradictory. But willful oblivion is a hallmark of Trumpian governance, and Mnuchin and his wife Linton have essentially become its "obtuse avatars," as *New York* magazine's Olivia Nuzzi puts it.[cxxxv] Whether by natural inclination or knowing calculation, Mnuchin's special blend of executive bootlicking and uninformed bluster has kept him in the president's good graces long enough to deliver some of the biggest items on Wall Street's wish list.

In one particularly shameful episode last August, Mnuchin rushed to defend the president's remarks that "both sides" shared blame for violence during neo-Nazi marches in Charlottesville, Virginia. After more than 300 former Yale classmates published an open letter calling for him to resign in protest, Mnuchin responded with a defiant public statement. "As someone who is Jewish, I believe I understand the long history of violence and hatred against the Jews (and other minorities) and circumstances that give rise to these sentiments and actions," he wrote, before acknowledging "different views of how history should be remembered" and asserting that "some of these issues are far more complicated than we are led to believe by the mass media."

Most Congressional Republicans, and even some members of the administration, sought to distance themselves from the president's remarks, but Mnuchin didn't blink. A *Washington Post* column later called him "the greatest sycophant in Cabinet history."[cxxxvi] Mnuchin's Treasury Department has slow-walked the release of financial records to the Senate committee investigating Russian meddling in the 2016 election, acting as a human shield to block additional Trump scandals.[cxxxvii] Another classic example came after the mass shooting in Parkland, Florida: Mnuchin told the House Ways and Means Committee "It's a tragedy what we've seen yesterday, and I urge Congress to look at these issues," and then immediately walked it back, lest anyone think he has an independent thought outside the wishes of the president on gun safety.[cxxxviii]

It's probably inevitable that someone this sycophantic will eventually lose standing with Trump; indeed, rumors emerged in November 2018 that Mnuchin was losing favor inside the White House.[cxxxix] But until then, blind loyalty appears to have kept him right where he wanted to be.

Mnuchin was Trump's key point person for tax reform in Congress, where he regularly bragged to members about his level of access to the president, according to a report in the *New York Times.*[cxl] The eventual passage of the tax bill didn't just put a feather in Mnuchin's cap, it put some serious money in the pockets of his friends on Wall Street: The nation's six largest banks saved $3.6B in taxes in the first quarter of

2018 alone.[cxli] In the second quarter, banks set all-time earnings records, thanks largely to the tax cuts.[cxlii]

Needless to say, it's bad news for most of us that Mnuchin is actually succeeding in implementing a policy agenda. Just how bad? In January 2018, an alarm bell sounded from an unlikely source--the International Monetary Fund, an organization that doesn't exactly have a tradition of left-wing activism. A report by economist Jihad Dagher examined the political economy of ten financial crises across the developed world, spanning 300 years, and shows how financial deregulation has historically been a prelude to meltdown.[cxliii] This works something like a pendulum: In 9 out of 10 examples, deregulation accelerated in the five years leading up to the crash, swinging back only after calamity had struck. Dagher even charts staffing levels at U.S. bank regulators during the past five decades, showing how they dwindle during booms and climb again after busts.

Yet the period of re-regulation following a crisis is often fragile. "Over time, the interest in financial regulation wanes, allowing the latter to decay and for regulators to be captured by concentrated private interests," Dagher writes.

We are now living in the period of decay. Mnuchin and his banker pals have given the pendulum a good shove, away from responsible oversight of the banking industry, and toward the kind of anything-goes chaos that led to the subprime mortgage collapse. It's not just that a handful of bank executives are rolling around in dollar bills thanks to Mnuchin's actions; it's that he's heading us directly into the path of the next financial crisis, putting our jobs, homes, and livelihoods at terrible risk.

If and when that crisis hits, you can bet it won't be Mnuchin and his friends who get the full force. Indeed, if recent history is our guide, they will likely find a way to profit at the expense of the rest of us.

As Mel Brooks once said in *History of the World Part I*: "It's good to be the king."[cxliv]

ABOUT THE AUTHORS

Rebecca Burns

Rebecca Burns is an investigative reporter whose work has appeared in the Baffler, the Chicago Reader, ProPublica Illinois, and The Intercept. Her coverage of Wall Street's role in the post-crash housing market won the Association of Alternative Newsmedia's first-place prize for investigative reporting in 2017. She is a dedicated Chicagoan and contributing editor at In These Times magazine.

David Dayen

David Dayen is a journalist who writes about economics and finance. He is the author of Chain of Title: How Three Ordinary Americans Uncovered Wall Street's Great Foreclosure Fraud, winner of the Studs and Ida Terkel Prize. He is an investigative fellow with In These Times and contributes to The Intercept, The New Republic, and the Los Angeles Times. His work has also appeared in The Nation, The American Prospect, Vice, The Huffington Post, and more. He has been a guest on MSNBC, CNN, Bloomberg, Al Jazeera, CNBC, NPR, and Pacifica Radio. He lives in Los Angeles.

End Notes

[i] https://www.washingtonpost.com/nation/2018/10/26/who-is-cesar-altieri-sayoc-what-we-know-about-suspected-mail-bomber-arrested-florida/?utm_term=.6eb6e5b4a607

[ii] https://twitter.com/MarcACaputo/status/1055889974439088128

[iii] https://drive.google.com/file/d/1wBTsiP5HPlhfvNMHclIwLG3Uta78TWRM/view

[iv] https://www.browardclerk.org/Web2/CaseSearch/Details/?caseid=NzQ3NDIy-U5ujoBpebYg%3d&caseNum=CACE09001136&category=CV

[v] http://fortune.com/2017/01/11/trump-cabinet-steven-mnuchin-net-worth/

[vi] https://www.irs.gov/pub/irs-soi/soi-a-ints-id1506.pdf

[vii] https://www.marketplace.org/2018/02/27/world/treasury-secretary-steven-mnuchin-conversation-kai-ryssdal

[viii] https://www.wsj.com/articles/mnuchin-dogged-by-protesters-doesnt-want-video-posted-1519849427?mod=rss_Politics_And_Policy

[ix] http://www.latimes.com/local/education/la-me-edu-ucla-mnuchin-video-20180313-story.html

[x] http://money.cnn.com/2017/11/15/news/louise-linton-steven-mnuchin-dollar-bills-treasury/index.html

[xi] http://thehill.com/homenews/sunday-talk-shows/361087-mnuchin-i-take-it-as-a-compliment-people-said-i-looked-like-a-bond

[xii] https://www.huffingtonpost.com/peter-dreier/steve-mnuchin-meet-rose-g_b_992940.html

[xiii] http://www.nydailynews.com/news/politics/steve-mnuchin-address-quiet-fear-protests-article-1.2893538

[xiv] https://theintercept.com/2017/01/19/treasury-pick-steve-mnuchin-denies-it-but-victims-describe-his-bank-as-a-foreclosure-machine/

[xv] https://www.finance.senate.gov/imo/media/doc/Mnuchin%20Confirmation%20Remarks%20-%20%20Final%2001182017.pdf

[xvi] https://www.nytimes.com/2016/11/30/business/dealbook/steven-mnuchin-is-more-pragmatist-than-ideologue.html

[xvii] https://www.yahoo.com/news/man-says-delivered-manure-mnuchin-protest-u-tax-231442875.html

[xviii] http://gawker.com/550099/bob-mnuchin

[xix] https://www.linkedin.com/in/alan-mnuchin-b344669/

[xx] http://www.thenewjournalatyale.com/2017/02/yale-men-cabinet/

[xxi] http://www.thenewjournalatyale.com/2017/02/yale-men-cabinet/

xxii http://www.pionline.com/article/20120224/ONLINE/120229909/hedge-fund-manager-lampert-gains-160-million-on-sears-shares-acquired-from-ziff-family

xxiii https://www.bloomberg.com/news/articles/2004-11-21/the-next-warren-buffett

xxiv http://www.thenewjournalatyale.com/2017/02/yale-men-cabinet/

xxv http://www.businessinsider.com/trumps-treasury-pick-mnuchin-and-sears-lampert-relationship-2017-1

xxvi https://www.vanityfair.com/news/2018/03/the-strange-odyssey-of-hedge-fund-king-eddie-lampert-sears-kmart

xxvii http://www.businessinsider.com/trumps-treasury-pick-mnuchin-and-sears-lampert-relationship-2017-1

xxviii http://www.thenewjournalatyale.com/2017/02/yale-men-cabinet/

xxix http://www.ifre.com/1977-us100m-deal-for-bank-of-america-the-first-private-label-mbs/21103057.fullarticle

xxx http://archive.fortune.com/2009/12/08/real_estate/lewie_ranieri_mortgages.fortune/index.htm

xxxi https://www.banking.senate.gov/newsroom/minority/brown-asks-trumps-treasury-nominee-to-explain-views-on-banking-housing-rules

xxxii https://www.nytimes.com/2000/11/16/business/michael-p-mortara-51-a-developer-of-mortgage-backed-securities.html

xxxiii https://www.bloomberg.com/news/articles/2016-05-05/trump-names-hedge-fund-manager-as-national-finance-chairman

xxxiv https://www.cnn.com/2018/03/26/politics/steve-mnuchin-chris-wallace-line-item-veto-congress/index.html

xxxv https://finance.yahoo.com/news/steve-mnuchin-goldman-sachs-royalty-and-culture-carrier-133523791.html

xxxvi https://uk.reuters.com/article/indymac/update-1-jc-flowers-others-close-to-indymac-deal-source-idUKN2829423720081229

xxxvii https://dealbreaker.com/2016/08/trump-steven-mnuchin-bloomberg-profile/

xxxviii https://www.forbes.com/sites/katevinton/2016/12/16/why-is-a-defunct-hedge-fund-listed-as-trumps-treasury-secretarys-main-job/#2a50b899104e

xxxix http://www.wsj.com/articles/before-politics-steven-mnuchin-was-hollywood-player-1480479252

xl https://www.imdb.com/title/tt1974420/fullcredits?ref_=tt_cl_sm#cast

xli http://money.cnn.com/2008/07/12/news/companies/indymac_fdic/

xlii http://www.nclc.org/images/pdf/pr-reports/report-servicers-modify.pdf

xliii https://www.menendez.senate.gov/news-and-events/press/menendez-demands-victims-of-mnuchin-foreclosure-machine-be-heard-during-treasury-confirmation-hearing

xliv https://thinkprogress.org/mnuchin-foreclosure-victims-b7675d134423#.hih4w2293

xlv https://www.youtube.com/watch?v=1R-E0Cxhj2Q&feature=youtu.be

xlvi https://www.treasury.gov/initiatives/financial-stability/reports/Documents/July%202013%20MHA%20Report%20Final.pdf

xlvii http://www.imdb.com/name/nm4373763/

xlviii http://nv.findacase.com/research/wfrmDocViewer.aspx/xq/fac.20121203_0005907.DNV.htm/qx

xlix https://apnews.com/0f1305c8742547df9bcf978b2c15997c

l http://blog.amerihopealliance.com/blog/bid/300236/5-Myths-About-HAMP-Loan-Modifications

li https://www.documentcloud.org/documents/3415447-Mnuchin-QFR-Response-01-22-2017.html

lii https://www.occ.gov/news-issuances/news-releases/2014/nr-occ-2014-65a.pdf

liii http://www.nakedcapitalism.com/2013/01/occ-foreclosure-file-reviewer-independent-reviews-were-controlled-by-banks-which-suppressed-any-findings-of-harm-to-foreclosed-homeowner.html

liv https://www.occ.gov/static/ots/misc-docs/consent-orders-97665.pdf

lv http://www.dictionary.com/browse/robosign

lvi http://4closurefraud.org/2009/11/15/full-deposition-of-the-infamous-erica-johnson-seck-re-indymac-federal-bank-fsb-plaintiff-vs-israel-a-machado-50-2008-ca-037322xxxx-mb/

lvii http://www.courts.state.ny.us/Reporter/3dseries/2010/2010_20429.htm

lviii http://www.reuters.com/article/us-foreclosure-banks-idUSTRE76H5XX20110718

lix http://www.dispatch.com/news/20170129/trump-treasury-pick-mnuchin-misled-senate-on-foreclosures-ohio-cases-show

lx http://4closurefraud.org/2009/11/15/full-deposition-of-the-infamous-erica-johnson-seck-re-indymac-federal-bank-fsb-plaintiff-vs-israel-a-machado-50-2008-ca-037322xxxx-mb/

lxi https://www.documentcloud.org/documents/3250383-OneWest-Package-Memo.html

lxii https://www.documentcloud.org/documents/3250384-OneWest-Sample-Complaint.html

lxiii https://www.documentcloud.org/documents/3250383-OneWest-Package-Memo.html

lxiv http://www.courts.ca.gov/1048.htm

lxv http://www.californiacityfinance.com/PropTransfTaxRates.pdf

lxvi http://www.nclc.org/images/pdf/foreclosure_mortgage/reverse-mortgages/ib-hecm-examples-loss-mitigation.pdf

lxvii http://money.cnn.com/2016/12/15/news/companies/mnuchin-reverse-mortgage-foreclosure/

lxviii https://badbankmerger.com/2016/07/07/onewest-bank-and-financial-freedom-have-foreclosed-on-16220-reverse-mortgages-since-2009/

lxix https://www.omm.com/our-firm/media-center/press-releases/omelvenys-brian-brooks-named-vice-chairman-of-onewest-bank/

lxx https://www.americanprogress.org/issues/economy/news/2017/01/18/296712/treasury-secretary-steve-mnuchins-bet-against-seniors/

lxxi http://dfw.cbslocal.com/2014/11/21/103-year-old-north-texas-woman-fights-to-keep-her-house/

lxxii http://www.nclc.org/images/pdf/foreclosure_mortgage/reverse-mortgages/ib-hecm-examples-loss-mitigation.pdf

lxxiii https://www.justice.gov/opa/pr/financial-freedom-settles-alleged-liability-servicing-federally-insured-reverse-mortgage

lxxiv https://www.federalreserve.gov/bankinforeg/citgroup-onewest-meeting-transcript-20150226_Part1.pdf

lxxv http://thehill.com/blogs/pundits-blog/finance/316758-foreclosure-fanatic-mnuchins-past-actions-make-him-unfit-to-serve

lxxvi https://www.bloomberg.com/news/articles/2016-12-13/mnuchin-s-reverse-mortgage-woes-blemish-record-of-treasury-pick

lxxvii https://democratsfinancialservices.house.gov/uploadedfiles/06.30.2017_onewest_letter_to_hensarling.pdf

lxxviii Ibid.

lxxix https://www.facebook.com/ReverseMortgageAdvocates

lxxx http://money.cnn.com/2016/11/30/investing/fannie-mae-freddie-mac-mnuchin-trump/?iid=EL

lxxxi https://www.forbes.com/sites/bisnow/2017/01/13/steve-mnuchin-trumps-treasury-pick-investment-could-benefit-from-fannie-and-freddie-restoration/#19cf58a810fc

lxxxii https://www.washingtonpost.com/news/wonk/wp/2017/05/19/trumps-pick-for-treasury-second-in-command-withdraws-from-consideration/?utm_term=.faa92a4afcd8 lxxxiii https://www.bloomberg.com/news/articles/2017-05-23/mnuchin-fills-top-jobs-at-treasury-by-avoiding-senate-scrutiny

lxxxiv http://www.creditslips.org/creditslips/2018/04/trumps-bank-regulators.html

lxxxv https://www.politico.com/story/2018/01/12/steven-mnuchins-ever-expanding-orbit-337493

lxxxvi https://www.nytimes.com/2017/04/07/business/fannie-mae-freddie-mac-craig-phillips.html

lxxxvii http://thehill.com/policy/finance/381344-trump-names-nominee-to-be-deputy-treasury-secretary

lxxxviii https://www.huffingtonpost.com/entry/joseph-otting-i-like-banks_us_5acbfb3fe4b07a3485e796e6

lxxxix https://www.americanbanker.com/news/not-just-wells-fargo-occ-finds-sales-practice-abuses-at-other-banks

xc https://www.politico.com/story/2018/06/07/drew-maloney-treasury-leaving-white-house-631547

xci https://www.wsj.com/articles/washingtons-500-million-financial-storm-forecaster-is-foundering-1519067903

xcii https://www.nytimes.com/2017/11/30/us/politics/treasury-analysis-tax-bill.html?_r=0

xciii http://www.chicagotribune.com/news/opinion/commentary/ct-perspec-taxes-farmers-estate-tax-family-farms-1116-story.html

xciv https://www.politico.com/story/2018/01/12/steven-mnuchins-ever-expanding-orbit-337493

xcv http://www.latimes.com/business/hiltzik/la-fi-3percent-20170519-story.html

xcvi https://www.bloomberg.com/news/articles/2017-12-01/economists-seem-to-back-off-economic-growth-claim-for-tax-cuts

xcvii https://www.cnbc.com/video/2018/04/17/treasurys-mnuchin-we-front-loaded-economic-growth-in-tax-plan.html

xcviii https://www.bea.gov/newsreleases/national/gdp/2018/pdf/gdp1q18_adv.pdf

xcix https://www.bea.gov/newsreleases/national/gdp/gdpnewsrelease.htm

c http://www.foxnews.com/politics/2018/07/29/mnuchin-us-definitely-headed-for-years-sustained-3-percent-growth-at-least.html

ci https://www.bloomberg.com/news/articles/2018-07-23/u-s-4-gdp-growth-seen-more-luck-of-the-draw-than-new-reality

cii https://www.cnbc.com/amp/2018/05/25/reuters-america-sp-500-companies-return-1-trillion-to-shareholders-in-tax-cut-surge.html

ciii https://www.axios.com/broad-based-pay-rises-retraining-automation-executives-3e68d31c-51bc-4bde-a362-7ce12b039e7c.html

[civ] https://www.bloomberg.com/news/articles/2018-01-31/mnuchin-met-with-apple-s-cook-ahead-of-first-tax-plan-release

[cv] http://money.cnn.com/2018/01/31/technology/microsoft-tax-charge-earnings/index.html

[cvi] https://theintercept.com/2017/07/08/trump-treasury-ripped-its-tax-cut-recommendations-straight-from-the-chamber-of-commerce/

[cvii] https://www.politico.com/story/2018/01/12/steven-mnuchins-ever-expanding-orbit-337493

[cviii] https://www.thedailybeast.com/trump-advisers-steve-mnuchin-and-peter-navarro-got-into-a-profanity-laced-screaming-match-on-the-china-trip

[cix] http://www.slate.com/blogs/xx_factor/2017/08/22/louise_linton_s_latest_instagram_post_makes_a_powerful_case_for_just_how.html

[cx] https://www.washingtonpost.com/news/wonk/wp/2017/09/14/mnuchin-eclipses-past-travel-backlash-with-pricey-request-european-honeymoon-by-military-jet

[cxi] https://www.vanityfair.com/news/2017/09/steven-mnuchin-honeymoon-plane

[cxii] https://www.citizensforethics.org/travels-treasury-secretary-steven-mnuchin/

[cxiii] https://www.washingtonpost.com/news/wonk/wp/2017/09/14/mnuchin-eclipses-past-travel-backlash-with-pricey-request-european-honeymoon-by-military-jet

[cxiv] https://thinkprogress.org/steve-mnuchin-had-fun-at-the-solar-eclipse-5d3c94388d45/

[cxv] https://theintercept.com/2017/05/18/steven-mnuchin-goes-through-the-looking-glass-steagall-in-strange-exchange-with-elizabeth-warren/

[cxvi] http://www.businessinsider.com/mnuchin-says-us-might-need-a-21st-century-glass-steagall-2017-1

[cxvii] http://www.vanityfair.com/news/2017/04/gary-cohn-glass-stegall

[cxviii] https://prod-cdn-static.gop.com/media/documents/DRAFT_12_FINAL%5B1%5D-ben_1468872234.pdf

[cxix] http://www.investopedia.com/articles/03/071603.asp

[cxx] https://www.bloomberg.com/news/articles/2017-05-16/forget-trump-s-breakup-talk-wall-street-is-writing-a-wish-list

[cxxi] https://www.treasury.gov/press-center/press-releases/Documents/A%20Financial%20System.pdf

[cxxii] https://www.treasury.gov/press-center/press-releases/Pages/sm0169.aspx

cxxiii https://finance.yahoo.com/news/federal-proposes-capital-rules-wall-street-013952935--sector.html

cxxiv https://prospect.org/article/banks-are-too-big-fail-say-conservatives

cxxv https://www.reuters.com/article/us-usa-banks-volcker-exclusive/exclusive-u-s-regulators-examine-wall-streets-volcker-rule-wish-list-sources-idUSKCN1GC1ZX

cxxvi https://www.wsj.com/articles/government-lifts-prohibition-on-payday-lending-chains-partnership-with-national-banks-1521233293

cxxvii https://www.reuters.com/article/usa-occ-lending/us-bank-regulator-encourages-banks-to-reconsider-small-dollar-lending-idUSL2N1SU159

cxxviii http://inthesetimes.com/working/entry/21351/trump_deregulation_fintech_occ_fcpb_mulvaney_finance_tech

cxxix https://home.treasury.gov/sites/default/files/2018-07/A-Financial-System-that-Creates-Economic-Opportunities---Nonbank-Financi....pdf

cxxx https://www.federalreserve.gov/newsevents/pressreleases/bcreg2014 0218a.htm

cxxxi https://www.revealnews.org/article/for-people-of-color-banks-are-shutting-the-door-to-homeownership/

cxxxii https://www.wsj.com/articles/cit-group-to-buy-onewest-profit-tops-estimates-1406025881

cxxxiii http://www.latimes.com/business/la-fi-onewest-redlining-20161115-story.html

cxxxiv https://www.wsj.com/articles/rewrite-of-low-income-lending-rules-faces-headwinds-1535112211

cxxxv http://nymag.com/daily/intelligencer/2018/02/the-misadventures-of-steven-mnuchin-and-louise-linton.html

cxxxvi https://www.washingtonpost.com/opinions/its-official-steven-mnuchin-is-the-greatest-sycophant-in-cabinet-history/2018/04/06/7f35069a-39b9-11e8-8fd2-49fe3c675a89_story.html

cxxxvii https://www.buzzfeednews.com/article/emmaloop/senate-intel-wants-to-follow-the-money-in-the-russia-probe?bftwnews&utm_term=4ldqpgc#4ldqpgc

cxxxviii https://www.vanityfair.com/news/2018/02/steve-mnuchin-rushes-to-clarify-he-doesnt-care-about-gun-laws

cxxxix https://www.wsj.com/articles/trump-expresses-dissatisfaction-with-treasury-secretary-1543006250?mod=hp_lead_pos2

cxl https://www.nytimes.com/2017/08/28/us/politics/trump-tax-plan-cohn-mnuchin.html

cxli https://apnews.com/96589643061e4437bd45fdcc35959fe0

cxlii http://thehill.com/policy/finance/403303-tax-cuts-help-us-banks-set-new-record-for-quarterly-revenue

cxliii https://www.imf.org/external/pubs/cat/longres.cfm?sk=45562.0

cxliv https://www.youtube.com/watch?v=StJS51d1Fzg

CPSIA information can be obtained
at www.ICGtesting.com
Printed in the USA
BVHW040219090119
537407BV00013B/231/P